DOES GOD HEAR ME WHEN I PRAY?

CHILDREN'S CHRISTIAN PRAYER BOOKS

BABY PROFESSOR

EDUCATION KIDS

Short Christian Prayers.

Practice reading and writing.

Angel of God, my
Guardian dear,
To whom God's love
commits me here;
Ever this day, be
at my side
To light and guard
To rule and guide. Amen.

Rewrite the paragraph.

Dear God,
Thank you for this day,
For fun, friendship
and family.
We give thanks
for this meal
And share our lives
always with you.

Rewrite the paragraph.

Trace the paragraph.

Thank you for the world
so sweet,
Thank you for the food
we eat,
Thank you for the birds
that sing,
Thank you God for
everything.

Rewrite the paragraph.

Dear Heavenly Father
from above,
Look down on (Names
of Children) with love,
Please keep them in
your care,
And tonight hear their
prayer.

Rewrite the paragraph.

God is great and
God is Good,
And we thank God
for our food,
By God's hand we must
be fed,
Give us Lord, our daily
bread. Amen.

Rewrite the paragraph.

Now I lay me down to sleep,
I pray the Lord my soul
to keep
If I should die before I wake
I pray the Lord my soul
to take
God bless our family
and our friends.

Rewrite the paragraph.

God in heaven hear
my prayer,
keep me in thy
loving care.
Be my guide in all I do,
Bless all those who
love me too.
Amen.

Rewrite the paragraph.

Now I lay me down
to sleep,
I pray the Lord my
soul to keep
May angels watch me
through the night and
wake me with the
morning light.

Rewrite the paragraph.

Dear God most high,
hear and bless
Thy beasts and singing
birds.
And guard with
tenderness
Small things that have
no words.

Rewrite the paragraph.

Trace the paragraph.

We thank Thee Lord,
for happy hearts,
For rain and sunny
weather.
We thank Thee, Lord,
for this our food,
And that we are
together.

Rewrite the paragraph.

Trace the paragraph.

Come Gracious Spirit,
Heavenly Dove,
With light and comfort
from above.
Be Thou our Guardian,
Thou our Guide,
Stay close by every
child's side. Amen!

Rewrite the paragraph.

Trace the paragraph.

We thank Thee Lord,
for happy hearts,
For rain and sunny
weather.
We thank Thee, Lord,
for this our food,
And that we are
together.

Rewrite the paragraph.

Trace the paragraph.

Dear God,
At the start of this
school day
Help us to learn and
help us to play
To concentrate on all we do
To understand and
remember too. Amen.

Rewrite the paragraph.

Dear Lord,
Thank you for this new day
Thank you for our school
Thank you for the teachers
Thank you for the
things we will learn
Thank you for the fun
we will have together.

Rewrite the paragraph.

Trace the paragraph.

Rewrite the paragraph.

Trace the paragraph.

Behold, God is my helper; the Lord is the upholder of my life. He will return the evil to my enemies; in your faithfulness put an end to them.

Rewrite the paragraph.

Trace the paragraph.

Guide me lord,

you are my heart

you are my strength,

you are my hope.

Teach me Lord, and

guide my way

I love you more each

passing day.

Rewrite the paragraph.

For this new morning with its light, For rest and shelter of the night, For health and food, for love and friends. For everything Thy goodness sends, We thank Thee, dearest Lord. Amen.

**Rewrite the paragraph.

Visit
BABY PROFESSOR
EDUCATION KIDS
www.BabyProfessorBooks.com
to download Free Baby Professor eBooks
and view our catalog of new and exciting
Children's Books